W9-BBC-419

**921
WAS**

3 24571 0900156 4
Raatma, Lucia.

**First of first
ladies : Martha
Washington**

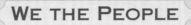

FIRST OF FIRST LADIES
MARTHA WASHINGTON

by Lucia Raatma

Content Adviser: Mary V. Thompson,
Research Historian, Mount Vernon Ladies' Association,
Mount Vernon, Virginia

Reading Adviser: Alexa L. Sandmann, Ed.D.,
Professor of Literacy, College and Graduate School
of Education, Health and Human Services,
Kent State University

Compass Point Books ✦ Minneapolis, Minnesota

Compass Point Books
151 Good Counsel Drive
P.O. Box 669
Mankato, MN 56002-0669

This book was manufactured with paper containing at least 10 percent post-consumer waste.

On the cover: Martha Washington visited Army headquarters at Morristown, New Jersey, in 1777.

Photographs ©: The New York Public Library/Art Resource, N.Y., cover, 35; White House Historical Association/White House Collection, 5; The Granger Collection, New York, 6, 7, 10, 11, 18, 19, 23, 26, 27, 31, 32 (all), 39; Line of Battle Enterprise, 9, 34; North Wind Picture Archives, 13, 17, 21, 28; The Bridgeman Art Library/Getty Images, 14; Library of Congress, 16, 38; Louis S. Glanzman/ National Geographic/Getty Images, 24; Bettmann/Corbis, 29; Jeremy R. Smith Sr./Shutterstock, 41.

Editor: Sue Vander Hook
Page Production: Bobbie Nuytten
Photo Researcher: Svetlana Zhurkin
Cartographer: XNR Productions, Inc.
Library Consultant: Kathleen Baxter

Art Director: LuAnn Ascheman-Adams
Creative Director: Joe Ewest
Editorial Director: Nick Healy
Managing Editor: Catherine Neitge

Library of Congress Cataloging-in-Publication Data
Raatma, Lucia.
    First of first ladies: Martha Washington / by Lucia Raatma.
        p. cm. — (We the people)
Includes index.
    ISBN: 978-0-7565-4125-5 (library binding)
    1. Washington, Martha, 1731–1802—Juvenile literature. 2. Presidents' spouses—United States—Biography—Juvenile literature. I. Title.
E312.19.W34R33 2009
973.4'1092—dc22
[B]   2008037633

Visit Compass Point Books on the Internet at *www.compasspointbooks.com*
or e-mail your request to *custserv@compasspointbooks.com*

Table of Contents

1 Lady Washington

"God bless Lady Washington!" the crowd cheered again and again. It was May 1789, and Martha Washington had just crossed the Hudson River on a fine barge. This was her day—the day she would begin serving as first lady of the newly formed United States of America. The people of New York City, the nation's capital at that time, welcomed her with cheers, shouts, and grand enthusiasm.

Martha's husband, George Washington, was also on the barge. New York had celebrated his arrival three weeks earlier. On April 30, 1789, Washington was inaugurated in New York City as the first president of the United States.

Americans had won the war against Great Britain, and the United States was a new nation. Now it was time for the first president and his wife to move into the house that Congress had rented for them. George Clinton, governor of New York, escorted the first lady and the president to their home at 3 Cherry St.

The nation had never had a president before. Lively debates arose about what to call him. Some thought His Serene Highness was a good title, but it sounded like British royalty. Americans didn't want to be like Great Britain, the country they had just defeated.

Martha Washington was 57 years old when she became first lady of the United States of America.

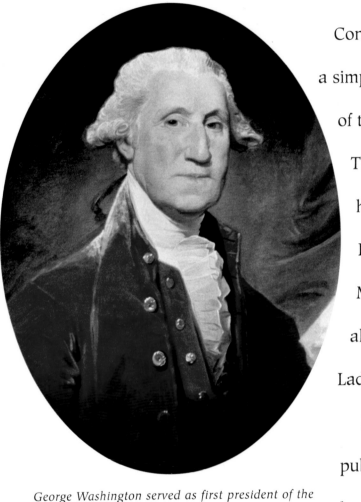

George Washington served as first president of the United States from 1789 to 1797.

Congress finally chose a simple title: President of the United States. They would address him simply as Mr. President. As for Martha, she was already known as Lady Washington. Martha disliked public life and would have preferred to be home in Mount Vernon, Virginia. But because she was duty-bound to her husband, she enthusiastically served the people of the United States. During her husband's presidency, Martha would plan many events and important dinners and welcome

Martha Washington held formal receptions that impressed the people of America, along with foreign leaders and other visitors.

hundreds of guests into their home. She would set a high standard as wife of the first president. Her commitment and grace would be a model for many other first ladies who would follow in her footsteps.

2 Young Martha

Martha Dandridge was born June 2, 1731, the first child

of John and Frances Dandridge. Seven more children would

eventually complete the Dandridge family.

Martha grew up in a two-story home called Chestnut

Grove in New Kent County, Virginia. It was situated on a large

plantation with sprawling fields of corn, cotton, and tobacco. Her

family owned slaves, who worked in the fields and in the house.

Slavery was common throughout all the American colonies in

the 1700s. Large plantations required many farmhands, and few

people questioned the practice of slavery.

John Dandridge was a good provider for his family and

gave his children a formal education. In those days, girls usu-

ally didn't go to school, but Dandridge made sure his daughters

learned reading, writing, math, and religion. A tutor came to the house to teach the boys, and the girls most likely learned a lot by listening to their brothers' lessons. Martha especially enjoyed music, dancing, horseback riding, and cooking. Sewing and embroidery were her specialties, and she learned to make nice clothes at a young age.

By the time Martha was 18, she was a charming, beautiful young woman. One person in particular—Daniel Parke Custis—was attracted to her. Although this wealthy Virginian was 20 years older,

Martha shopped in nearby Williamsburg, where she bought dresses and accessories.

they fell in love and were married May 15, 1750. The couple moved to a huge 17,500-acre (7,000-hectare) estate that Custis had inherited from his father. Their house, known as White House, was nestled on the banks of the Pamunkey River, not far from where Martha grew up.

Daniel Parke Custis was Martha Washington's first husband.

Martha and Daniel lived a lavish lifestyle—expensive clothes, fine furniture, and fancy parties. But the years to come would be filled with sorrow. In 1751, Martha delivered their first child—a boy named Daniel Parke, after his father. Two years later a daughter, Frances Parke, was born. But the following year, young Daniel died at the age of 3. Martha and Daniel were grief-stricken, and Martha became very protective of Frances.

In 1754, not long after young Daniel's death, Martha gave birth to another son, John Parke Custis. They called him "Jacky." Two years later, in 1756, another daughter, Martha Parke Custis, was born. Her nick-name was "Patsy."

Martha most likely stayed busy caring for three children under the age of 5. But one year later, in 1757, tragedy again struck

John "Jacky" Parke Custis and Martha "Patsy" Parke Custis

the Custis household. Martha's worst fears came true when 4-year-old Frances became ill and died. Later that year, Martha's husband also became very ill and died. Suddenly 26-year-old Martha Dandridge Custis was a widow, alone with two children to raise.

Although deeply distraught, Martha remained strong. She concentrated on taking care of little Jacky and Patsy, and worked hard to keep White House running smoothly. Her husband had left a great deal of property and wealth. Now it was hers, and she focused on managing his estate. But in less than a year, her life would again change dramatically.

3 Becoming Mrs. Washington

*I*n March 1758, Martha Dandridge Custis met a tall military man named George Washington. He was quite well known for his military exploits for the British army during the French and Indian War (1754–1763). At that time, the American colonies were governed by Great Britain.

George and Martha enjoyed each other's company. George visited Martha regularly at her home and got to know young Jacky and Patsy. The

George Washington served in the British army until 1758.

visits ended, however, when George was ordered back to the battlefield. But before he left, he asked Martha to marry him, and she accepted.

It was December before they saw each other again. George had resigned from the military and was preparing Mount Vernon, his Virginia home, for his bride-to-be. On January 6, 1759, Martha Dandridge Custis and George Washington were married at White House. Martha's tragedies and difficult life were now replaced with happiness and hope for the future.

Martha Dandridge Custis and George Washington were married in Virginia in 1759.

In April, George and Martha moved to Mount Vernon. It was difficult for Martha to leave White House and her relatives and friends. But she soon felt comfortable at beautiful Mount Vernon with its stunning view of the Potomac River.

Martha spent her days caring for 4-year-old Jacky and 2-year-old Patsy. It was also her job to oversee the cook and the maids, as well as supervise the garden, the chickens, and the dairy cattle. She also managed the children's schooling by hiring a tutor to come to Mount Vernon. Ensuring that Jacky and Patsy got a good education was important.

The Mount Vernon plantation was quite large, with orchards of fruit trees and herds of cattle, horses, and sheep. Martha taught slaves how to spin wool and make fine cloth out of flax. She put her sewing talent to good use and taught Patsy and some of the slave girls how to mend and make clothes for the slaves.

Mount Vernon overlooks the Potomac River in Fairfax County, Virginia, about 15 miles (24 kilometers) south of Washington, D.C.

Throughout the years, Martha and George had a strong relationship. George welcomed Martha's opinions on how to run the plantation, and Martha didn't hesitate to offer advice about supplies, crops, and servants. However, their views on raising children were sometimes different. George thought Martha was over-protective and spoiled the children. Martha was indeed over-protective, but she had good reason to worry. Two of her children had died, and Patsy often had seizures.

Martha Washington was in charge of Mount Vernon's domestic slaves, who worked as maids, seamstresses, cooks, and waiters.

In the coming years, Martha would have more to worry about than just her children. The American colonies would soon demand their freedom from England, and the Washingtons would play key roles in making sure that freedom was won.

4 The American Revolution

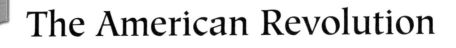

By the 1760s, the relationship between the American colonies and Great Britain had grown very unpleasant. The British government needed money and began charging taxes on goods that came into the colonies. The British also passed the Stamp Act of 1765. It required colonists to buy stamps, a type of tax, for all their documents, including newspapers, diplomas, bills, and even playing cards.

The colonists argued that the taxes were unfair. After all,

The American colonists held protests and demonstrated against the Stamp Act of 1765.

they had no voice in the British Parliament. The British eventually repealed the Stamp Act but then taxed glass, paper, tea, and other products. The colonists were furious. George Washington urged the people of Virginia to boycott British goods. He said it would prevent England from collecting taxes and show the British that the colonists would not be mistreated.

Martha Washington disliked the idea of giving up British tea and other fine goods, but she supported the boycott wholeheartedly. On March 5, 1770, the colonists' anger over taxation

Minutes of a Boston town meeting described plans for a boycott against British imports.

erupted in a clash with British soldiers on the streets of Boston, Massachusetts. Five colonists died at what came to be known as the Boston Massacre.

In the midst of growing concern over British rule, tragedy again struck the Washington home. In June 1773, 17-year-old Patsy had another seizure, but this time she died. Martha was heartbroken. George wrote, "This sudden and unexpected blow, I scarce need add has almost reduced my poor wife to the lowest ebb of misery." Jacky, who was away at college, returned home to help his mother. Martha now had just one living child. She mourned her losses deeply and found it hard to be joyful about anything. Even Jacky's upcoming marriage to Eleanor "Nelly" Calvert the following year would not rid Martha of her sorrow. When Jacky and Nelly married in 1774, George went alone to his stepson's wedding. Martha was too grief-stricken to attend.

All the while, problems between England and the colonies

were growing worse. Two months before, on December 16, 1773,

a group of colonists had dumped a huge amount of British tea

into Boston Harbor, an event that came to be called the Boston

Tea Party.

It was the colonists' way of protesting the tax on tea, and it

In protest against British taxes, colonists dressed up like Native Americans and dumped 45 tons (40.8 metric tons) of tea into Boston Harbor.

enraged the British government. Great Britain reacted by passing several laws; the colonists called them the Intolerable Acts. The laws closed down the port at Boston, required colonists to provide free food and housing for British soldiers, and generally gave Britain more control over the colonies. With every new law, the colonists grew angrier.

In August 1774, George Washington left Mount Vernon to attend the First Continental Congress in Philadelphia. Colonists met to discuss unfair taxation and plan a boycott. Martha worried about what would happen if the colonies decided to stand up to England. On April 19, 1775, her fears came true. Shots were fired in Lexington and Concord, Massachusetts, marking the beginning of the Revolutionary War between the colonies and Great Britain.

A month later, George Washington gathered with other patriot leaders at the Second Continental Congress. In June, the

Congress formed the Continental Army and appointed George

Washington as commander.

Martha tried to keep busy while George was away with

the Army. Family members and friends visited her to keep up her

spirits. In October, George asked her to spend the winter with

him. Two months later she set out with Jacky and his wife, Nelly,

On June 15, 1775, at the Second Continental Congress, George Washington accepted the appointment as commander of the Continental Army.

for Cambridge, Massachusetts, the Army's winter headquarters.

Church bells rang and people cheered when she passed through

their towns. They knew she was the wife of their commander,

and they wanted to encourage her

on her winter journey.

Martha wasn't prepared for

what she saw along the way—a

violent and deadly war. Martha

wrote to a friend, "I confess I

shudder every time I hear the

sound of a gun." George was grate-

ful to have his wife with him. He

shared his problems with her,

and she helped him in any way

she could. She mended clothes,

treated soldiers' wounds, and did

Martha traveled in harsh winter weather to visit George at Army headquarters.

her best to cheer up the troops. Two officers' wives, Lucy Knox and Catharine "Kitty" Greene, brought a cheerful optimism to the camp with their singing and dancing.

Somehow the Continental Army made it through that first winter. By spring 1776, they forced the British out of Boston. On July 4, the Continental Congress approved the Declaration of Independence. It was the colonies' announcement to the world that they intended to become an independent nation—free of England's rule.

By the middle of September, the British took control of New York City. In December and January, Washington and his troops rallied and defeated the British at Trenton and Princeton, New Jersey. Then they camped nearby for the winter. Martha, now back at Mount Vernon, worked hard to provide clothing for the soldiers. She put her servants and other women to work spinning wool, weaving cloth, knitting socks, and making uniforms.

*George Washington and his troops watched as British forces,
under the command of General William Howe, fled Boston, Massachusetts.*

One of the women wrote about Martha: "She seems very wise in experience, kind-hearted and winning in all her ways. She talked much of the poor soldiers, especially the sick ones. Her heart seems to be full of compassion for them."

As the war continued, both sides scored victories. However, the Continental Army was ill-equipped and often lacked food, clothing, and supplies. By the time they arrived at Valley Forge, Pennsylvania, in December 1777, the troops were exhausted, and their uniforms were wet and ragged. They set up camp for the winter and tried to stay warm in the extreme cold of the cruel months that followed. Soldiers slept in makeshift log huts. Food, water, and blankets were scarce, and many became ill from smallpox and other diseases. George Washington worried that all his men might die.

In February 1778, Martha arrived at Valley Forge and immediately got to work. She and other women made more uniforms. Daily Martha walked about the camp, listening to soldiers'

The Continental Army spent the winter of 1777–1778 at Valley Forge, Pennsylvania; the harsh conditions made it a time of great suffering.

Martha Washington was shocked at the poor conditions at Valley Forge.

worries and fears and offering them emotional support.

More than 3,000 soldiers died that winter. But more than 6,000 survived, encouraged to hang on by the determination of George Washington and the compassion and hope of his wife, Martha. It would be three more years before the fighting would be over. Martha would spend two more winters in the Continental Army's camps.

5

A New Nation

*I*n May 1778, the colonists learned that France was joining them in their battle for independence. Yet as the years went on, Army supplies ran low and conditions for the soldiers got worse. In June 1780, Martha Washington joined the Ladies' Association to help raise money for the Army. The women visited and wrote to other women throughout the colonies to encourage them to support the troops. In a few months, they collected about $300,000 from women

The Ladies' Association of Philadelphia met regularly to sew shirts for the Continental Army.

29

in Philadelphia alone. Martha donated $20,000 of her own money as part of Virginia's contribution.

In 1781, the Continental Army won some battles but also suffered some defeats. But when the Battle of Yorktown ended, British General Charles Cornwallis surrendered. It would prove to be an important victory for the Americans.

As everyone was enjoying the victory, tragedy again struck the Washingtons. Jacky, now 27, had gone to the Battle of Yorktown with his stepfather but had come down with a high fever. Two weeks later, at the home of nearby relatives, Jacky died. With Jacky gone, Martha had now lost all her children. Her daughter-in-law, Nelly, had four children to raise on her own: Elizabeth ("Betsy"), Martha ("Patty"), Eleanor ("Nelly"), and George Washington Parke ("Washy").

Two years after the Battle of Yorktown, British and American officials signed a peace treaty. On September 3, 1783,

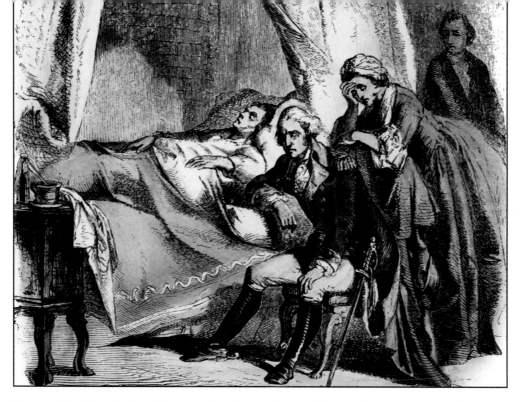

Two weeks after the British surrendered at Yorktown, the Washingtons mourned the loss of Martha's son, John "Jacky" Parke Custis.

the American Revolution was officially over. In December, George Washington resigned as commander in chief of the Continental Army.

Martha and George now poured their energy into Mount Vernon. They got the plantation back in good shape and began entertaining family and friends. Late in 1783, Nelly married Dr. David Stuart. Nelly's two oldest children, Betsy and Patty, lived with them, while 4-year-old Nelly and 2-year-old Washy stayed

Eleanor "Nelly" Parke Custis

George Washington "Washy" Parke Custis

at Mount Vernon to be raised by their grandparents. The Washingtons were thrilled to have the little ones to take care of.

In the meantime, the people of the United States began to consider what kind of government they would have. In the spring and summer of 1787, George Washington attended the Constitutional Convention in Philadelphia. Representatives from all 13 states drafted and approved the U.S. Constitution. Two years later, the country elected the first president of the United States of America—George Washington.

6

First Lady

Martha Washington was proud of her husband and understood his strong sense of duty to his country. Although she longed for a quiet life at Mount Vernon, she knew she must go with her husband to New York City, the capital of the new nation. Martha was devoted to her husband and committed to her country.

She wrote to her friend Mercy Otis Warren: "I cannot blame him for having acted according to his ideas of duty in obeying the voice of his country. I am still determined to be cheerful and to be happy, in whatever situation I may be."

George Washington was inaugurated as the first president of the United States on April 30, 1789. Martha was not at the inauguration or the magnificent ball several days later. She was at Mount Vernon, packing and preparing to leave.

When everything was organized, Martha set out for New York City with 10-year-old Nelly and 8-year-old Washy. As she traveled through cities and towns, people cheered, church bells rang, fireworks exploded, and bands blared. Martha Washington was already a heroine—part of the reason the Americans had won the war.

As she settled in as first lady, Martha established traditions and set high standards. She became good friends with Abigail Adams, wife of Vice President John Adams. Together the two women planned elegant dinners and events for visiting leaders.

Martha Washington served as first lady of the United States from 1789 to 1797.

Martha sometimes found formal parties too stiff, so she created weekly receptions called levees. In Europe levees were formal ceremonies held for royalty when they got up in the morning, but Martha planned a new kind of levee—for all Americans. Each Friday the Washingtons welcomed people—all kinds of people—to their home on Cherry Street. Anyone could come, as

Martha Washington hosted weekly social events at her home in New York City.

long as they were dressed properly. Common citizens and sol-diers came in droves to get to know their president and first lady.

In 1790, the capital of the United States was moved from New York City to Philadelphia. Martha was more at home in this city and enjoyed shopping and going to the theater. And she continued the weekly levees. Now the president and first lady got to know the people of Philadelphia.

After four years in office, George Washington would have quietly left the presidency, but leaders convinced him to run for a second term. Martha had been looking forward to going home, but she accepted her husband's decision to run again.

George Washington was elected for a second term. Four years later, Congress pleaded with him to run yet again. But Washington said no. Although there were no laws at that time limiting how long a president could serve, Washington was ready to let someone else lead the country. That person was John

Adams. His vice president was Thomas Jefferson.

Martha could finally go home to Mount Vernon, although

life was not as quiet there as it used to be. Almost daily, Martha

and George entertained visitors—regular citizens, former soldiers,

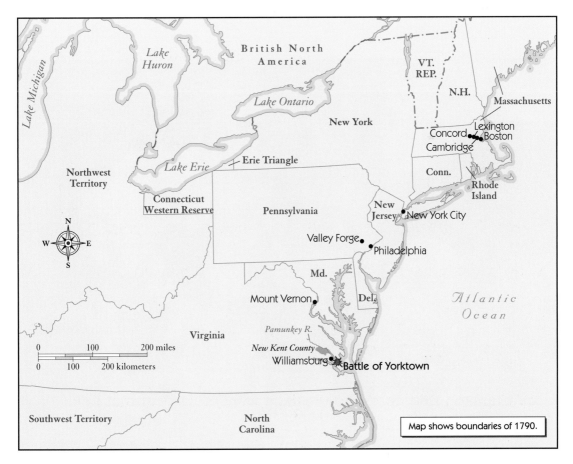

Martha Washington spent most of her life in Virginia. She also lived in New York and Pennsylvania.

world leaders. Martha also spent a great deal of time with her grandchildren. Joy surrounded her as weddings took place and great-grandchildren were born.

However, the Washingtons' happy home life ended December 14, 1799, when 67-year-old George Washington died.

Visitors were always welcome at Mount Vernon, where Martha and George lived with their two grandchildren.

Martha said, "All is now over, I shall soon follow him. I have no more trials to pass through." The nation honored their first leader at his funeral on December 18. However, Martha was not there; she was too sad to attend.

For the next two and a half years, Martha tried to lead

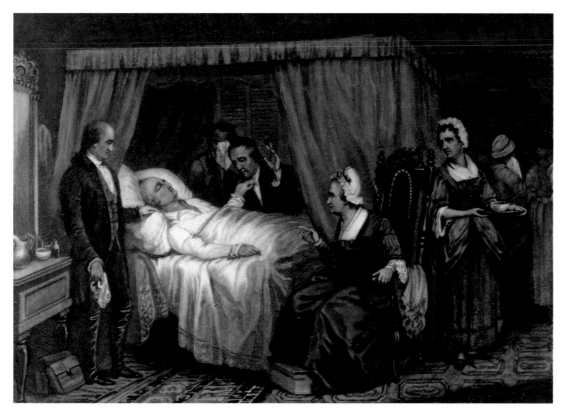

Martha Washington was at her husband's bedside when he died at Mount Vernon on December 14, 1799.

a normal life, but she missed her husband terribly. She closed off George's study and the bedroom they had shared and never entered either of them again. She moved to a smaller third-floor bedroom where she spent time praying, sewing, and sleeping.

Family members and friends stayed close to Martha during those years. She still entertained guests and worked on knitting and sewing projects from time to time. And she enjoyed her grandchildren and great-grandchildren. But in May 1802, illness confined Martha to her bed for 17 days.

She planned her funeral and gave advice to her loved ones. On May 22, 1802, 70-year-old Martha Washington died. Her body was placed alongside her husband's in a tomb at Mount Vernon. News spread quickly of Lady Washington's death. Newspapers hailed her as "the worthy partner of the worthiest of men."

Martha Washington is still remembered as a worthy

Daily wreath-laying ceremonies take place from April to October at the tomb of Martha and George Washington.

woman who gave up much of her personal life to serve her country. She supported her husband when he was leader of the Continental Army, offering her time and talents to provide clothing, encouragement, and money for soldiers.

Finally, she served as a gracious and dedicated first lady. Although her husband was the head of the United States, it has been said that Martha Washington was the heart of the nation.

Glossary

boycott—refusal to buy certain goods or services as a form of protest

colonies—lands settled by people from another country and controlled by that country; the 13 American colonies were controlled by England

constitution—document stating the basic laws of a state or nation

inaugurate—swear in as a public official

intolerable—describing something that is hard to tolerate, endure, or live with

Parliament—part of the British government that makes laws

patriots—American colonists who wanted freedom from England's rule

repealed—officially canceled, such as a law or tax

seizures—sudden attacks that make a person shake violently

taxes—fees that people and businesses must pay to support a government

treaty—agreement signed between people or countries

tutor—teacher who gives private lessons

Did You Know?

- When Martha Washington arrived in New York City in 1789, it is said she wore a dress made of homespun cloth, made in the United States of America. At the inauguration of George Washington three weeks earlier, he wore an American-made brown suit. The Washingtons were making a silent statement that they were not a king and queen. Instead they were "made in America" and servants of the people.

- When Abigail Adams first met Martha Washington, she was very impressed. In a letter to her sister, Abigail described Martha: "She is plain in her dress. … Her hair is white, her teeth beautiful, her person rather short than otherways. … Her manners are modest and unassuming, dignified and feminine, not the tincture [trace] of hauteur [arrogance] about her."

- During the winter of 1777–1778 at Valley Forge, Army officers rented local farmhouses as their residences and offices. When Martha Washington came to Valley Forge, she stayed with her husband in a rented house owned by Isaac Potts. There George coordinated the war effort and received local and foreign leaders. Martha and other officers' wives often used the home for social events and entertainment to lift the soldiers' spirits.

- After George Washington died, Martha burned almost all the letters they had written to each other during their 40 years of marriage. Perhaps this was a way to keep part of their lives private forever.

Timeline

1731	Born June 2 in New Kent County, Virginia, near Williamsburg
1750	Marries Daniel Parke Custis on May 15
1751	Son Daniel Parke Custis is born
1753	Daughter Frances Parke Custis is born
1754	Son Daniel dies at age 3; son John "Jacky" Parke Custis is born
1756	Daughter Martha "Patsy" Parke Custis is born
1757	Daughter Frances dies at age 4; husband Daniel dies
1759	Marries George Washington; moves to Mount Vernon
1778	Arrives in February at Army headquarters at Valley Forge, Pennsylvania
1789	Becomes first lady of the United States; moves to the nation's capital in New York City
1790	Moves to nation's new capital in Philadelphia, Pennsylvania
1799	Husband George Washington dies December 14 at Mount Vernon
1802	Dies May 22; entombed next to her husband, George, at Mount Vernon

Important People

Daniel Parke Custis (1711–1757)
Virginia planter and first husband of Martha Washington from 1750 until his death in 1757; he died at 45 one of the wealthiest men in the colony.

Eleanor "Nelly" Parke Custis Lewis (1779–1852)
Martha Washington's granddaughter whom she raised after the death of her son John "Jacky" Parke Custis; Nelly helped her grandmother entertain guests at the presidential residence in Philadelphia and at Mount Vernon; married George Washington's nephew Lawrence Lewis

George Washington (1732–1799)
Martha Washington's second husband; commander of the Continental Army, who led the American colonies to victory over Great Britain in the American Revolutionary War (1775–1783); presided over the Philadelphia Constitutional Convention that drafted the U.S. Constitution in 1787; became first president of the Unites States in 1789; served two terms

George Washington Parke Custis (1781–1857)
Martha Washington's grandson by her first marriage to Daniel Parke Custis; raised by Martha and George Washington at Mount Vernon; he became a noted writer and playwright.

Want to Know More?

More Books to Read

Allen, Thomas B. *Remember Valley Forge: Patriots, Tories, and Redcoats Tell Their Stories*. Washington, D.C.: National Geographic, 2007.

Burgan, Michael. *George Washington*. Minneapolis: Compass Point Books, 2002.

Burgan, Michael. *Valley Forge*. Minneapolis: Compass Point Books, 2004.

Murray, Stuart. *American Revolution*. New York: DK Publishing, 2005.

Simon, Charnan. *Martha Dandridge Custis Washington, 1731–1802*. New York: Children's Press, 2000.

On the Web

For more information on this topic, use FactHound.

1. Go to *www.facthound.com*

2. Choose your grade level.

3. Begin your search.

This book's ID number is 9780756541255

FactHound will find the best sites for you.

On the Road

Mount Vernon
3200 George Washington
  Memorial Highway
Mount Vernon, VA 22121
703/780-2000
Plantation home and burial
place of George and Martha
Washington; includes house,
slave quarters, stables, green-
house, and gardens

**Valley Forge National
Historical Park**
Route 23 and North Gulph Road
Valley Forge, PA 19482
610/783-1077
Site where the Continental
Army endured the winter of
1777–1778, near Valley Forge,
Pennsylvania

Look for more We the People Biographies:

American Patriot: Benjamin Franklin

Civil War Spy: Elizabeth Van Lew

Confederate Commander: General Robert E. Lee

Confederate General: Stonewall Jackson

A Signer for Independence: John Hancock

Soldier and Founder: Alexander Hamilton

Union General and 18th President: Ulysses S. Grant

A complete list of We the People titles is available on our Web site:
www.compasspointbooks.com

Index

About the Author

Lucia Raatma loves learning about people's lives and writing about them. In addition to biographies, she has written books about history, safety, animals, and character education. She has a bachelor's degree in English from the University of South Carolina and a master's degree in cinema studies from New York University. When she is not writing or reading, she enjoys going to movies and spending time with her husband, their two children, and their golden retriever.